AMAZON
ECHO DOT
USER GUIDE
FOR **NEWCOMERS**

Echo Dot help manual: guide to Echo Dot troubleshooting, tricks, and using Alexa

Stephen W. Rock

Dedicated to all my readers

Acknowledgement

Ii want to say a very big thank you to Michael Lime, a 3D builder, my colleague. He gave me moral support throughout the process of writing this book.

Table of Contents

Introduction

The title of this book already gives a hint on what the book is about. It is a guide for new users of the Amazon Echo Dot: 2nd and 3rd generation.

Readers will be introduced into the Echo Dot proper, learn Echo Dot set up and operation and be taught through basic Echo Dot troubleshooting.

Also, readers will learn how to configure and customize the Echo Dot to perform several impressive actions, including but not limited to streaming music, reading books, using Echo Dot with IFTTT, controlling home appliances, shopping on Amazon, etc.

Eventually, you'll come to when you'll see several Alexa commands for TV, music and Easter eggs.

The content of this book are well presented. Steps are outlined to make it easier for readers to identify what to do and how to go about it without any distraction.

This is just another superb user guide from the author's stable. Read and explore.

CHPATER ONE

How To Setup Echo Dot

The first thing you'll need to do with your brand new Amazon Echo Dot is to set it up. So how do you go about this? Carefully consider the following steps:

Setup from the Echo Dot

So as you get your Echo Dot, of course you're going to open up the box. Inside the box that your Echo Dot comes in, you'll find these items

1. The Echo Dot itself (of course)

2. For the powering unit, you get a micro USB cable

3. Power adapter

4. A Starter guide

5. Card containing some Alexa commands

To start off, you'll want to first connect the microUSB cable to your Echo Dot. Once you've connected that, you now want to plug the other end of the cable to the power adapter which in turn you'll plug to a socket on the wall.

Also you want to make sure that your Dot is the center of the room so that it can hear and listen to your voice from anyplace. You don't have to worry about the microphones much they are known to be solid.

To show that it has started, it will show a blue light. Once this happen, you want to wait for a while for the Echo to go through its initialization procedure. And as soon as an orange light appears, Alexa will tell you can go online.

Setup from your phone

As you know already, the Echo Dot does not have a screen. So to finish up the setup, you'll have to do it from your phone. But when you do it from your phone, you want to be sure to use the appropriate store to download the Alexa app.

- For Android users, it's **Amazon Alexa**
- For iOS, it's **Amazon Alexa**
- And for those who don't have a smartphone, they can make use of **Alexa web portal**

After you've gotten the app from the appropriate app store for your device,

1. You download and install the app.

2. After installation, go to your app list and open up the **Alexa app** you just installed.

3. Then you'll be prompted to sign in to your account. If you don't have an Amazon account, you'll be asked to create one. And it might even pick out your Amazon account if you have the Amazon app already.

4. After signing in, you'll need to accept the terms of use.

5. You'll now see different Echo devices, but select the Echo Dot since that's what you want to set up.

6. Select a language and Connect to Wi-Fi

7. Your Dot should be in orange now if you've plugged it in

8. Hit **Continue**

Now your phone will make an attempt to find the Echo Dot. It should find it but if it doesn't, press the action button on your Echo for a while and once it's found, select **Continue**. The next thing to do is to include your Dot to your Wi-Fi network. Select the name of your network from here and put it the password. Hit **Connect** and your Echo should go online.

That not all, you still need to select how you would like to listen to your Echo Dot. You'll be given 3 selections to choose from.

- Audio Cable
- Bluetooth
- No Speakers

With this you'll have the ability to connect your device to speakers with an Audio cable or you could go through the Bluetooth route. If you don't actually fancy those options, you can just easily select the last option of **No Speakers**. If you choose this, the audio will be played via the speakers of the Dot

Now you can rejoice, you completed the setup. But the Alexa app will throw you a video on how you can use Alexa. And you will be prompted to either Decline or Accept **Prime music** and **Amazon Prime** free trial.

Connecting your Echo Dot to Bluetooth devices

Of all the things you'll love to do with your Echo Dot, connecting it to Bluetooth devices cannot be excluded from the list. We will touch two mandatory Bluetooth devices; **Echo Dot speakers** and **Echo Dot mobile devices**.

Connecting your Echo Dot to Speakers

Of course you know that you can listen to audio from your Echo Dot. But you can amp up the quality and connect it to speakers, you don't have to be confined to your Dot. You have the ability to listen to music from Mars far away from Alexa

If you're still looking to buy speakers, you want to first check out Amazon's website for speakers that are compatible with your Echo Dot. You don't want to spend millions only for you to find out that, well, it doesn't work with your Dot.

If you've gotten yourself a Bluetooth speaker, let's get connecting

1. First of before we start pressing or tapping any settings, you want to first put your speakers and Echo 3 feet apart at the very least
2. Your device can connect to more than one Bluetooth device at a time. So you want to be sure to disconnect any devices that are connected to your Echo

3. Put your Bluetooth speaker on, increase the volume and put it in pairing mode

4. Open up the **Alexa app** and navigate to the **Devices icon**

5. Choose the your Echo Dot that you wish to pair with the speaker

6. Then **Bluetooth devices**

7. Choose **Pair a New Device** and as the list of devices show up, choose your speaker.

8. You'll be notified when connection is complete

Connecting your Echo Dot to Mobile devices

With your Bluetooth enabled Echo Dot, you can stream audio directly from your tablet or smartphone. But before you start connecting, there are a few things you want to make sure of.

- And you want to remember that your Echo Dot can connect to just one Bluetooth device at a specific time.
- You want to verify that your mobile device accepts the Bluetooth profile that your Dot knows.
- You want to put your mobile device on and should be in pairing mode. It should also be close to your Echo Dot
- And also, you want to note that Alexa does not accept text messages or phone calls from your phone

To start the pairing

1. Open up the **Alexa app** on your mobile device
2. Enter the let navigation pane and choose settings
3. Choose your Echo dot
4. Then **Bluetooth**

5. Choose **Pair a New Device**, and your Dot should be in pairing mode

6. On your mobile device, go to the **Bluetooth settings** and tap your Echo Dot. If you don't see your Echo Dot, you may have to wait for a few seconds before it shows up. If the notification is successful, you'll be notified by Alexa

7. Say '**Disconnect**' to disconnect your Echo Dot from your device

Once you've made it through the first connection, all you just have to do the next time is to put your Bluetooth on the mobile device say the word '**Connect**'

CHAPTER TWO

Using Echo Dot with IFTTT

If you have no idea what IFTTT means, then it's stands for **If This Then That**. That helps you make conditional 'statements or recipes' that performs specific actions that you set

1. Go to **IFTTT** and Enter the **Alexa channel**
2. If don't have an IFTTT account, create one. If you do, sign in
3. Then **Connect**
4. After signing to you Amazon account, permit IFTTT to sync with your Alexa account

Or use recipes

1. In the **Alexa options,** select an applet you wish to use
2. To enable a recipe, Hit **Turn On**
3. Start making use of the applets by carrying out the trigger.

Using Echo Dot with different types of skills

You can get very used to your Echo Dot, it runs with Alexa so you can tell it commands. But without skills Alexa will not effective. And by skills, I mean apps that make Alexa to link to the Echo Dot and do task.

There are certain skills that you don't have to enable them before they are enabled. Once you use the skill it be enabled automatically.

Here are a few of Alexa skills

Sleep sounds
Want to hear sleep sounds before you sleep, you can get Alexa to do that for. You get different sounds for you to fall asleep
To use this, say **'Alexa, open Sleep sounds'**

Push Up century club
Want to increase your number of push-ups? Just get Alexa to open up Push Up century club. This gives a foundation for fitness starting from the level you're at.
To use this, say **'Alexa, start push-ups'**

Spotify

This is said to be a top music skill for Alexa devices. One thing about Spotify is that it allows you set it as a default service. You can do this via the Alexa app.

To use this, say **'Alexa, play (say music) from Spotify'**

Science Buddy

This is basically a quiz around different subjects and topics like biology and earth science.

To use this, say **'Alexa, open Science Buddy'**

Spelling bee

This one is to test spelling knowledge. Have a kid? Test out his spelling ability with this skill, You can even ask for definition of words, or to use in a sentence.

To use this, say **'Alexa, open Spelling Bee'**

The Bartender

A favorite skill of many. This allow you to tell Alexa how you can make a cocktail and it will tell you the ingredients you need

To use this, say **'Alexa, enable The Bartender'**

Reuters TV

For those who want a rundown of the news for the day, Reuters TV s a great option. With this you can have a selection for a flash briefing each morning

To use this, say **'Alexa, what's my flash briefing'**

ESPN

Okay sport lovers, this one's for you. You get a wide selection of sports. Is it touchdowns, goals, or slam dunks name it, you get them here

To use this, say **'Alexa, what's my Flash briefing'**

Creating Alexa routines

You can make use of the Alexa app to create Routines that set how your Echo Dot and other smart home devices work

Of you want to create a routine with your phone or tablet via the Alex app

1. Enter the **Menu**
2. Choose **Routines**
3. You should see the plus (+) icon at the upper right
4. Tap **When this happens.** With this, you'll be able to select how to activate the routine
5. To choose what action this does, choose **Add action**
6. To choose the device that controls this, go to **From**
7. Hi **Create**

If you want to delete a routine, go to the Alexa app again and the **Routines.** In the Enabled segment, select the routine. You can also do this is you just want to modify the routine

CHAPTER THREE

Giving Commands to Echo Dot like a Pro

There are a plethora of commands that can be given to your Echo Dot device; from asking Alexa to play songs with the lyrics to finding Alexa skills. We will consider all the commands needed to explore your Echo Dot.

Play song with the lyrics

Okay let's say you know this song. You know it pretty well, but it's been kind of long since you listened to it so you've forgotten some part of the lyrics, but you know they said something like

"The only one who makes me smile in the Pacific"

All you just Is say **'Alexa, play the song that goes like (say the lyrics you know)'** and you hear Alexa say **'Life so long' by Kesteeh Blues.**

Check on the weather

Let's say you're on your couch and you want check the weather. Sure you can use phone, but it's far away in bedroom.

Just say **'Alexa, what's the weather going to like this morning'**

Measure distance

Want to know how far you'll be travelling, use Alexa. The assistant can use GPS to give you the driving distance from your current location to your destination. Alexa is pretty brilliant, don't you think?

You can say **'Alexa, how far is florenta from home'**

Translation

I would love to say that Alexa can translate what you say to **any** language on earth but then the assistant can work in a couple of languages.

If you want to know if a particular language is available, first say **'Alexa, open translated'** then **'Alexa, how to you say Thank You in Spanish**

Calculations

Not all of know how to subtract and add big numbers in a split second. You can just ask Alexa.

Say something along the lines of **'Alexa, how much is $945 plus $68.56**

Conversions

Alexa can be a huge life saver in this case. Want to convert something really quickly, just say

'Alexa, what is 583 miles in kilometers?'

Alarm

Set alarms quickly by saying something like

'Alexa, wake me up at 7 a.m.'

Get flattery

A little fun with the assistant won't be bad. You can feed your ego and say

'Alexa, flatter me' what you hear should make you crack a smile.

Notifications

Are your hands so busy you can't even tap on your phone to see notifications?

You could say **'Alexa, what did I miss?'**

Find skills

If you want to hear a few more skills say

'Alexa, new skills' and you should get 3 new skills from Alexa

CHAPTER FOUR

Shopping on Amazon with Echo Dot

Through your Alexa app, you can make purchases from Amazon if you have your device is Alexa enabled. You can even use voice purchasing to but items from Amazon.

After registering your Alexa device, the voice purchasing setting is automatically enabled. If you sense that it is not enabled and you want to enable it or it's annoying you and you want to disable it,

1. Open up the **Alexa app**

2. Enter the **Menu**

3. Choose **Settings**

4. Then **Alexa Account**

5. Select **voice purchasing**

6. From here you'll be able to manage the option to turn on of turn it off.

Of you disable it, you want be able to purchase by voice. But you can still do other things like tracking of your orders and adding to cart.

Shopping for physical and digital products

First thing to do is to enter your information

1. Enter the amazon website

2. Select the **Account & Lists** tab. This will enable to be able to sign in to your account

3. If you have an account already, just sign in normally. But it's ur first time, Click the option **Start here**

4. Enter your information in the form it presents to create your account

5. Now to add your sipping address
   - Go to **Your Account**
   - Choose the **Address Book**
   - Select **Add new address** in settings

6. To add your billing information
   - Go to **Your Account**
   - Then **Manage Payment Options**
   - Choose **Add New Payment**

To find a product digital or physical,

1. Click the long search bar in the Amazon website

2. With this, you can search for whatever product you want

3. Once you see an item you would like to buy, click it and it will open the page of the

product which comprises of description, reviews and other details

4. Click on the option titled **Add to Cart**

5. To complete your purchase, click on the **Cart icon** and it will show all the items you've ordered

6. Click the **Proceed to checkout** option at the left part of the page

7. From here you'll be able to choose shipping address, choose your payment method

8. Click the place your order option when you're done with your order

9. To track and manage your order, Amazon will send an email to you

CAPTER FIVE

Using smart home devices with Echo Dot

You want to first install Alexa skills for the device that you want to link to your Echo. If you install these skills, the syncing will be effective with virtually any brand.

To install

1. Go to **Alexa app**
2. Then **Skills**
3. Select your brand
4. Follow the process it takes you through

After setting up the devices, you want to link them with Alexa

1. Enter the **Alexa app**
2. Go to **Smart home**
3. Then hit the plus (+) button at the upper right
4. Using the skills you just installed and home network, Alexa should find the device

Some commands to get you started with your lights

- **'Alexa, lights off'**
- **'Alexa, Set light to blue'**
- **'Alexa, make the light cooler'**
- **'Alexa, dim lights to 60%'**
- **'Alexa, lights on'**
- **'Alexa, set light to soft white'**

Programming Echo to Control Lights, Thermostat and Door Locks

If you cannot program your Echo Dot to control lights, thermostats and door locks, then you are underutilizing the Echo Dot. So, how then can you use the Echo Dot in respect to the three things mentioned? Let's quickly get into the next subheading.

Programming echo to control lights

As long as you've connected your smart tights to your Wi-Fi, you can control them with your Amazon Echo. Once you connect your smart lights to your Echo, you just have to tell Alexa to control your lights

1. Open up the **Alexa app**
2. Enter the **Menu**

3. Choose **Smart home**

4. Select **add Device** and your device should be discovered by Alexa

5. Check your device list for the smart light that's been added recently

Programming echo to control Thermostat

We have heard of controlling your thermostat with your phone which is nice and all but I think controlling with your voice is way cooler. It's just like those actions we watch in sci-fi movies coming to reality.

If you've got an Echo and you use a smart thermostat, it's time you switch things up and connect them. You can do some very interesting things with the combo

To add to you Echo,

1. Head over to the **Alexa app**
2. Enter the **Menu**
3. Choose **Smart home**
4. Slide downwards and select the arrow next to the option titled **Get More Smart Home Skills**
5. Type in the name of your thermostat (**Ecobee3, Nest**). The logo of your thermostat should show up now
6. Select **Enable Skill**
7. Sign in to your thermostat brand's account
8. Choose **Accept**

Programming echo to control Door locks

You can now tell Alexa to lock your doors. How convenient. Those nights when you're half asleep then you remember that you've forgotten to lock your front door you just tell Alexa to do it for you while you continue sleeping.

You want to connect your ZigBee or Z-wave locks to your smart home hub. Also set names for your doors that you can remember.

You would need smart locks that are compatible like **Kiwiset, Smart things**, and of course your **Echo**

Once you connect, you need to enable the skill through the Alexa app

1. In the **Alexa app**, go to **Settings**
2. Select **Skills**
3. Then **Smart things** and **enable**

4. Then you will have to tell Alexa to 'Discover new devices'

CHAPTER SIX

Getting customized weather, traffic, and news updates

If you want to get weather forecast, news or other updates daily, just set up your Echo to enable **Flash briefing**.

Using **Flash briefing** is just as easy as saying, 'Alexa, what's my Flash briefing?' You should hear Alexa say the news service that is part of your flash briefing. This news service could be Associated Press or CNN or other services.

If you want to customize or modify your Flash briefing or to include more skills

1. Fire up the **Alexa app**
2. Select the Flash briefing that Alexa newly gave in the home screen
3. Hit the **More icon**
4. And to see the link for you to able to customize

You can get and enable various skills from the flash briefing home screen. If you need to get more sills just choose the selection that will allow you to get more Flash briefing content

Get Alexa to tell you a joke

You would think Alexa only has a serious side to her with no jokes. But actually the assistant is quite humorous – that is if you are capable of bringing out the humor in her.

And when I say capable, I don't mean the regular **Tell Me a Joke** line. That gets old very fast as she will reply with some plain joke. If you view that as funny, well that's only a scratch on the surface.

If you really want to get some puns from the assistant, you've got to do more than just tell her to do so. You've got to ask some sneaky questions. Can't think of any right now, not to worry, we've got you covered.

Alexa jokes

'Alexa, what is the value of pi'
She would say 'The estimated value of pi is 3.1415926535........... (then say 'this thing goes on forever')

'Alexa, will you be my girlfriend

'I like you but as a friend'

Alexa can you give me some money
(this answer fluctuates an there is no one answer,
but one is) 'The thing about clouds is there are
no pockets and no pocket means no wallet'

Alexa do you have any pets
'I have some bugs. But they kept getting
squashed'

'Alexa, how much do you weigh
'I'm weightless like clouds. Wait, clouds weigh a
lot. Let just say that I am more sass than a mass.'

Alexa what do think about Cortana
'I like Cortana. We both have experience with
light right but hers is more of a Halo'

'Alexa, how old are you

She would say different jokes. Some of the jokes would be rhymes. Others would be discussions about how Artificial intelligence calculate years in nanoseconds

'Alexa, drop a beat'
You should hear her giving you a beat

'Alexa, the cake is a lie
'No the cake is not a lie. It's delicious. You can have some after asking me questions'

'Alexa, rap for me
You would hear various responses to this question. But many of them are about how she is better and faster. Should certainly make you crack a smile.

'Alexa, sing a song
She sings you different songs

Try out a few yourself and hear what she says

'Alexa, how old is Santa Claus?'

'Alexa, can I tell you a secret?'

'Alexa, who is your best friend?'

'Alexa, are you evil?'

'Alexa, am I funny?'

'Alexa, what is happiness?'

'Alexa, rock paper scissors'

'Alexa, when is the end of the world?'

'Alexa, where do babies come from?'

'Alexa, I think you're funny'

'Alexa, see you later, alligator'

'Alexa, good night'

'Alexa, do you have brothers and sisters?'

'Alexa, what is your feature?'

'Alexa, do you smoke?'

'Alexa, what size of shoe do you wear?'

CHAPTER SEVEN

Getting latest news from your favourite team

First of all, you want to check if the league you're interested in is supported. Yes, you should say that that Alexa supports wide variety of sports and leagues, but not all. These leagues are supported

MLS, NBA, NFL, WNBA, MLN, NCAA, NHL.

English Premier League, German Bundesliga, FA Cup, UEFA Champions League

Then to get Alexa to tell you the latest score lines, you could just say **'Alexa, what were today's scores?'** Alexa should reply with information about games, like the current score of a game that's played at the moment or any sport games that's has been played. You can even request for a specific team or day and the ones that will play next.

Things you could say are:

Alexa what were Sunday's scores?

Alexa, give me NBA scores from Monday

Alexa, give me NFL scores

Alexa, how did the Bulls do?

To set up your favourite team,

1. Fire up the **Alexa app**

2. Hit the **menu icon**

3. Select **Settings**

4. Choose **Traffic**

5. Then **Sports update**

6. Press the search to search for your team

7. From the option that appears, choose you team

8. If you want Alexa to provide you with latest games and also the dates for the games that have not yet been played, you can say **'Alexa, give me my sports update'**

How to change Alexa voice

We will discuss how you can alter Alexa's voice and change it to a different accent. Sadly for those who would like to choose a male voice for Alexa, it's not possible. All the voices Alexa has are all female.

But in terms of accent, you can change them to Canadian, English (UK), US, Indian or Australian. If you change Alexa voice, it will reduce her ability to recognize your voice – that is if you don't speak the particular accent you chose.

To do this,

1. Launch the **Alexa App.**

2. Then **Settings**

3. From here you'll be able to choose the device that you want to modify. If you have not yet changed the name of your device, you should see Echo Dot or Echo depending on what you use.

4. Move down and select the option for **Language** with your current language shown underneath

5. From the list of languages or accent, choose the one you wish to change it to.

6. Then **Save Changes**

7. Hit **Yes** and **Confirm**

Don't forget that if you don't speak the accent of the language you've just changed it to, Alexa may not recognize your voice. If you've changed it and Alexa's having a hard time understanding you, try to mimic and copy the accent of the language you've chosen.

If you speak other languages, you have the option of select ether Japanese or German. Unfortunately, these are the only options available or a different language. We can only hope that there will be an upgrade in the future to include several other languages.

But you can try this out and choose any of the languages if you can speak them. And if you are still learning, it can just be a good way to hone your skills in the language.
If you wish to change Alexa's voice back to the way it was, you can just follow the same process.

Change Alexa name

If you're the type that doesn't like to follow the rest of the sheep and use the same mundane thing they are using, you can do the same with your Echo. You can change Alexa's name. Maybe you don't like the sound of Alexa itself.

Or it could be that is your pet's name. Imagine how awkward it will get when you say 'Alexa, come get your lunch' (you should totally try it and hear what Amazon Alexa will say). You wouldn't want to start explaining yourself to Amazon Alexa, so just change her name. It's not that you can change the name for everyone worldwide. It's just what you say wake her up from your Echo.

I would wholeheartedly love to say that you can change Alexa's name to whatever you want. But that is not the case. Amazon only gave us 3 options to choose from. And it's just the basic names, nothing fun (Echo, Amazon, Computer). I'm still here racking my head why they didn't make it so we can type in whatever we want. Then we could put something like Buddy or Chum.

If you're still interested in changing her name,

1. Go to the **Alexa app**
2. Then hit the **menu icon**
3. Choose **Settings**
4. Select the device you want to change the name for
5. Move downwards and choose **Wake word**
6. Press **Alexa Device wake word** and choose your preferred name
7. Hit **Save**

CHAPTER EIGHT

Using Pre-Tested Commands and Easter Eggs

You've just gotten your Echo or Echo Dot. But you're quite unsure of what to say to Alexa. It's normal, we are all used to talking to human beings, not voice assistants. So when you first get your Echo, may find that you really don't know what to tell it.

Well here are some commands to tell to Alexa and get you started with your Echo

Music commands

'Alexa, pair my phone'

'Alexa, turn this off in 5 minutes'

'Alexa, play RnB

'Alexa, play the latest of **Katy Perry**'

'Alexa, set the volume to 4'

'Alexa, create a (input name) playlist'

'Alexa, louder'

'Alexa, play (say the name of playlist) from (say the music service)

'Alexa, who is singing this song'

'Alexa, play **Friday morning music**'

Basics

'Alexa, set timer for 7 minutes'

'Alexa, set an alarm for 6 a.m.'

'Alexa, what's the weather going to be like today?'

'Alexa, play (say radio station name)

TV commands

'Alexa, open up Netflix'

'Alexa, fast forward 8 minutes'

'Alexa, tell me the IMDb rating for **Man From The Snow**

'Alexa, turn down the volume on Fire TV'

'Alexa, play next episode'

'Alexa, tell me all about the movie **The Great Hunter**'

'Alexa, show movies with **Dwayne Johnson**'

'Alexa, who stars in **Ground Adventure**?'

'Alexa, play (movie title)'

'Alexa, pause'

Reminders and calendars

'Alexa, add and event on calendar

'Alexa, what am I doing today'

'Alexa, tell me what's on my to-do list'

'Alexa, add features meeting to calendar on Monday at 2:00'

'Alexa, what's on my schedule?'

'Alexa, add do dishes to my to-do list

EQ controls

'Alexa, set night mode'

'Alexa, set night mode on living room TV'

'Alexa, set bass to 5 on sound bar'

'Alexa, decrees the bass in bedroom'

'Alexa, set treble to 5'

'Alexa, set to movie mode'

'Alexa, increase the treble'

'Alexa, decrease the bass'

Timers and Alarm

'Alexa, wake me up every day at 4:00 a.m.

'Alexa, snooze'

'Alexa, set alarm for 7:00 a.m.'

'Alexa, set timer for 8 minutes'

'Alexa, stop timer'

'Alexa, how long left on the timer'

'Alexa, set a 9 minute burrito timer

'Alexa, wake me up at 5 a.m. to (say radio station name or a music title)

Smart home devices

'Alexa, set temperature to 19'

'Alexa, lock the garage door'

'Alexa, lights on'

'Alexa, discover my devices' (do this to discover your smart home devices)

'Alexa, lights out'

'Alexa, turn on the TV'

'Alexa, trigger (name for IFFT recipe) recipe

'Set the light to white'

'Alexa, dim the light to 70 percent'

CHAPTER NINE

Easter Eggs

Now let's cook some eggs. Okay not literal eggs, they are just something like secret commands you can dish out to Alexa that can make you laugh or just bring out the not so serious side of her. Want to try it out, let's get cooking then,

'Alexa, why so serious'

'Alexa, it is a trap'

'Alexa, are you able to talk like Yoda'

'Alexa, where do babies come from?'

"Alexa, tell why the chicken crossed the road'

'Alexa, will pigs ever fly?'

'Alexa, tell me where you are from'

'Alexa, is Siri better than you?'

'Alexa, can you rap for me?'

'Alexa, are you talking to me?'

'Alexa, beam me up'

'Alexa, more cowbell'

'Alexa, what is in a name?'

'Alexa, do you like pizza?'

'Alexa, take me to you leader'

'Alexa, did you just fart?'

'Alexa, tell me the sound that a hamster makes?

'Alexa, do you think there is Mars?

'Alexa, high five'

'Alexa, tell me are you a nerd?'

'Alexa, what are you really thinking about?'

CHAPTER TEN

Stream music and read books on Echo Dot

Your Echo Dot is a great way to turn your home into a smart home. But not only can it work to control your smart home devices, it can also play music and read you books, Cool right?. You don't need to have the full Echo, the Dot too is capable of being a good music player.

But you need be aware of something. Yeah it's true you can listen to music from your Echo Dot, but it's only good as a basic speaker. So if you really want to enjoy your music will all the beats and inner instruments, you might want to connect to an external speaker. You'll get the audio much clearer

Using prime for music

When you subscribe to Amazon prime, you get a lot of perks. One on them worth mentioning now is the **Prime music**. This prime music is a music streaming service that comprises of some 2 million songs. It also includes Alexa music stations.

If you download music it will be added to your account right away. And once it's added, you can stream them with your Echo Dot without any hassle.

1. Fire up Amazon Music player web interface

2. On the left side spot and select the option to **Upload your music to your cloud library**

3. From here you'll be able to download the **Amazon music player app** and install it

To play the music from your Dot say these

'Alexa, play my music'

'Alexa, play classical music'

'Alexa, play prime music that is for dancing'

'Alexa, play the top Jazz station'

Other music services

You can also use third-party music services on your Echo Dot if you don't prefer the Prime music. But you'll have to connect your accounts if you want to listen to music and songs from these thirty party music services.

1. Launch the **Alexa app** in your phone or tablet
2. Then **menu icon**
3. Choose **Settings**
4. Then under the **Accounts** segment, select **Music & media**

You should have connected your Amazon account with the **Amazon music** entry. From here you are able to connect your different music accounts. Like Pandora, iHeartRadio, Spotify or even TuneIn Radio

After you've signed in for them, go to the bottom of the page and select the button for **Choose default music service**. With this, you'll be able to choose the radio station or music library that you prefer.

If you want Alexa to play something from a music service, you can say,

'Alexa, play Tree Drifters radio on Pandora'

'Alexa, who is this artiste?'

'Alexa, play the station MKTW45'

Using Alexa to read kindle books

You have the ability of asking Alexa to help you read out certain books that are eligible in your content library. If the book supports text-to-speech, Alexa can read it.

You can look for books that are eligible in the Alexa app for her to play.

1. Hit the **Play** icon
2. Choose a book that's in the carousel from the kindle library
3. From the dropdown menu, select a device

You can say

'Alexa, play the kindle book **The Man and the grey lady**

'Alexa, pause'

'Alexa, skip'

CHAPTER ELEVEN

Controlling Your Home Appliances Using Echo Dot

There are many devices out there that you can get and control them with your Echo Dot. Is it Lights, garage doors, thermostats, fans or even air-conditioners? You can link them to the internet and then you'll be able to give commands to them with your Echo Dot.

So you will need

- An assistant, of course it's **Alexa**.
- A reliable piece of hardware, you already have it, your **Echo Dot**
- Smart home devices

Lights

There are lot of smart lights in the market so finding one won't be hard.

- Download the app of your bulb, if you're using a smart Lifx bulb, you'll want to install the Lifx app on your phone.
- Connect your bulb to a Wi-Fi network and give it a name, let's say 'beam'
- Fire up the **Alexa app**
- Enter the **menu** and choose **Skills**
- Look for the skill of the brand of your lights and enable
- Now on the **menu**, tap **Smart home**
- Choose **Devices** and then **Discover** for the app to look for your lights you named 'beam'

Fans and others

There are many other appliances that you'll have to plug in for them to work 'smartly'. Like electric water, kettle, fans and even coffee makers. What's even cooler is that is when you plug them to a smart plug, you can use Alexa to set a particular time for them to do certain things like to heat the water in the kettle during the mornings.

You'll need a smart plug and a plug-in fan with a power switch that will remain in the **on** spot

1. Download the app of your smart plug and register through the app
2. After connecting the smart plug to an outlet, plug your fan to the smart plug.
3. In the smart plug app, follow the instruction to sync your phone with the smart plug

4. Enter the app of your smart plug and give your bulb a name. Put the remote control option on and follow the directions given for you to connect the smart plug to Wi-Fi

5. Open the **Alexa app,** enter the menu and select skills

6. Search for your smart plugs skill and **enable**

7. In the **menu,** choose **Smart home**

8. Select **Devices** and then **Discover** for Alexa app to find the smart plug

Do More With Routines and Make Alexa Smarter

Routines can be really beneficial. It makes Alexa work like a real assistant. Like for example you don't have to tell your real assistant to get you a coffee and to bring in the document, then to sign in the report? They know they should do those stuffs when they see you in the morning.

Same with Alexa, you don't have to say 'Alexa, do this' 'Alexa, do that' you can just set it that any time you say 'Alexa, good night' she'll turn off your lights, play a soft underground music, lock your doors, condition your thermostat and tell you **sleep tight.**

1. Open up the **Alexa app**
2. Select the **menu icon**
3. Then **Routines**
4. Hit the **plus** button
5. Then you'll see an option for **when this happens.**
6. If you select this you'll be presented with different options
   - **Voice** will start the routine. You can a word or phrase that you want like

'Alexa, goodnight' that we mentioned earlier

- With **Schedule**, it will trigger the routine during the days or the time you set. You can also choose only weekdays or weekends
- **Device** will start the routine with a motion sensor. You would need something like Smart Things
- **Arrive or Leave** will use the location of your smartphone to trigger the routine like at work or other places
- **Echo Button** would need Amazons big button

To setup the triggers you just choose of the them from the options it gives and then follow the directions it gives you.

You can also make the routine to trigger at only specific times by tapping **Change** beside the segment for **Anytime** and set it up. This option is for **Arrive or Leave, Echo Button** and **Device**

Once you've setup the trigger, if you want other actions to follow it, you can just select the button for **Add action.** Once you tap that, you'll be presented with different options

CHAPTER TWELVE

Troubleshooting Echo Dot

You are welcome to the final chapter of this users guide. Learning to troubleshoot your Echo Dot is a skill you'll always appreciate you knew. There a few troubleshooting advice that are contained in this text. They are the most common issues that disturb the Amazon Echo Dot device. What are they? How can they be resolved? Consider the suggestions below.

Echo Dot doesn't turn on

You Dot might refuse to turn on. Or may not reply to the commands you give it.

1. Check the power cord. You may not have plugged it the right way. Make sure you insert it inside the port completely. Also check if the power outlet where you plugged the power adapter is working

2. Check if the wires of the power are worn or visible and showing. If you find that there's a problem with the power cord, change it

Bluetooth doesn't connect

1. Before you start panicking, how about you draw Echo closer to your Bluetooth device. Should be at least 3 feet distance.

2. Check the Bluetooth settings of your device

3. If your device is not connected your Echo Dot, just say 'Alexa, pair' and choose Echo in the settings

Alexa cannot understand my commands

1. Don't say complex words, try to make it simple
2. There might me an interference, don't put your Echo Dot too close to the wall or near other devices that may interfere

Doesn't connect to Wi-Fi

1. Bring your Echo Dot closer to your router, and move other devices that may cause interference away
2. Make sure to enter the Wi-Fi password properly and correctly
3. Try turn off you router and after a few seconds, turn it back on.

Activating by itself

1. Check your command triggers for your Echo Dot. There may be too many that even a slight noise from outside can make Alexa respond

2. Move to a quieter spot. Maybe the noise in your current location is too much

3. Reset your Echo by Holding down the Volume down key and microphone off key

CONCLUSION

The guide you just finished reading is from the stable of the **Newcomers** series. The Echo Dot is about the best Echo from Amazon. In this text, it has been explained how to set up the Echo Dot, connect it to Bluetooth devices, shop on Amazon, connect it with home appliances and execute several Alexa commands.

The suggested Alexa commands in this text are numerous; from music commands, to TV commands, to Easter eggs.

The last subject discussed revolves around troubleshooting an Echo Dot device. Hopefully, you learned a lot from reading this text.

Disclaimer

In as much as the author believes beginners will find this book helpful in learning how to use an Echo Dot device, it is only a small book. It should not be relied upon solely for all Echo Dot tricks and troubleshooting.

About the author

Stephen Rock has been a certified apps developer and tech researcher for more than 12 years. Some of his 'how to' guides have appeared in a handful of international journals and tech blogs. He loves rabbits.

Facebook page @ Newcomers Guide

Also by the Author

1. IPHONE USER MANUAL FOR NEWCOMERS: All in one iOS 12 guide for beginners and seniors (iPhone, 8, X, XS & XS Max user guide)\
2. APPLE WATCH USER GUIDE FOR NEWCOMERS: The unofficial Apple Watch series 4 user manual for beginners and seniors
3. 3D PRINTING GUIDE FOR NEWCOMERS
4. SAMSUNG GALAXY S9 PLUS USER MANUAL FOR NEWCOMERS
5. WINDOWS 10 USER MANUAL
6. KINDLE FIRE HD MANUAL FOR NEWCOMERS

S

www.ingramcontent.com/pod-product-compliance
Lightning Source LLC
Chambersburg PA
CBHW031246050326
40690CB00007B/974